johnson banks

La collection design&designer est éditée par
PYRAMYD ntcv
15, rue de Turbigo
75002 Paris – France

Tél. : 33 (0) 1 40 26 00 99
Fax : 33 (0) 1 40 26 00 79
www.pyramyd-editions.com

Direction éditoriale : Michel Chanaud, Patrick Morin, Céline Remechido
Traduction : Étienne Menu
Correction français : Alexandra Roy
Correction anglais : Paul Jones
Conception graphique de la collection : Super Cinq
Conception graphique du livre : Pierre Klipfel
Conception graphique de la couverture : Pyramyd ntcv
Portraits de la couverture : Ulf Andersen

ISBN : 2-35017-004-7
ISSN : 1636-8150
Dépôt légal : 1er semestre 2005
Imprimé en Italie par Eurografica

johnson banks

préfacé par alan fletcher

NOTES PERSONNELLES AU SUJET D'UN CONFRÈRE

Michael Johnson est un danger public. Je le suspecte de ne jamais trop savoir dans quelle direction il s'engage lorsqu'il commence un projet. Je ne sais pas si cette attitude – non dénuée, hâtons-nous de le souligner, d'un charme imprévisible – provient de ses origines sociales, d'une inclination personnelle ou d'une disposition génétique. Bien sûr, cela pourrait également signifier que lui-même ne sait pas ce qu'il fait, ou encore que je n'ai rien compris à sa manière d'envisager les choses.

Je le soupçonne d'avoir reçu une bonne éducation, bien que les informations sur son enfance soient confidentielles. Ce soupçon se fonde sur son aisance d'expression et sa capacité d'apprentissage et, si j'ose dire, sur ses bonnes manières. Certes, j'ai bien lu quelque part qu'il était diplômé en marketing et en arts visuels d'une université à Lancaster. Ou peut-être était-ce même la Lancaster University. Au nord de l'Angleterre. Cet indice nous prouve au moins qu'il sait ce qu'il fait.

Ses premières expériences professionnelles furent aussi aventureuses que bénéfiques ; il fit ses premières armes dans le métier comme un moussaillon gagne ses gallons. Tout commença lorsque, pour une raison inexplicable, il s'exila en Australie « car [il] avai[t] besoin de devenir graphiste » – projet pour le moins singulier, s'il en est. Vous voyez à quoi je faisais allusion quand je disais qu'il

PERSONAL NOTES ON A COLLEAGUE

Michael Johnson is a loose cannon. I suspect that when he embarks on a project he's never quite sure in which direction he will end up pointing. I'm not sure whether this characteristic, which, I hasten to add, has its own unpredictable charm, is the legacy of his social background, of his personal inclination or of genetic disposition. It could, of course, equally signify he doesn't know what he's doing or that I haven't figured out how he goes about things.

I suspect he received a good education although information on early life is kept private. This impression is based on his articulate and knowledgeable personality and, dare I say it, good manners. I did read somewhere that he graduated in Marketing and Visual Art from a university in Lancaster. Or maybe it was the University of Lancaster. That's in the north of England. Well at least that indicates he knows what he's doing.

His early work experience was adventurously gained in a deckhand manner. I think it all started when,

ne sait jamais trop vers où il va. Cela dit, cette décision se révéla moins improbable que prévu. Michael Johnson passa trois ans à l'autre bout du monde, travaillant à Melbourne, à Sydney, au Japon, avant de revenir chez lui via New York.

De retour à Londres, ses premières années comme designer consistèrent en plusieurs courtes expériences au sein d'agences de création et d'institutions, comme Wolff Olins, Sedley Place et Smith & Milton, pour n'en mentionner que trois. Aucun de ces trois établissements ne saurait être considéré comme un fief de la pensée Max Bill/Armin Hoffman/Muller Brockman, et encore moins de Weingart's. Ce ne sont pas davantage des sympathisants de l'école de New York, incarnée par le trio Dorfsman/Rand/Lubalin. Johnson a appris à travailler dur, avec ses mains, dans des studios de base, pas dans des salons de spéculation philosophique.

Si je tiens à faire ce constat, c'est que le travail de Michael ne correspond ni à une posture idéologique, ni à une conviction personnelle. Aucun mal à cela ; il n'en demeure pas moins, selon moi, que son rôle relève plus du DA pragmatique que du designer consciencieux à l'excès. Il travaille moins par petites touches méticuleuses que par grands aplats, ce qui ne veut pas dire pour autant que son travail est dépourvu de style : disons simplement qu'il préfère les amples mouvements symphoniques au solo de piccolo. En lisant cela, vous devez vous demander pourquoi j'ai décrit Michael

for some inexplicable reason, he thought of going to Australia as "I needed to be a graphic designer". That's a weird notion if ever I heard one. You see what I mean by pointing in the right direction. Paradoxically, it wasn't such an odd idea. It propelled him around the world on a three year stint working for a while in Melbourne, Sydney and Japan, and a return journey via New York.

His formative years in design practice after he returned to London included brief spells at various creation hothouses and institutions. Wolff Olins, Sedley Place and Smith & Milton, to mention three. None of which could be described as ideological havens of the Max Bill/Armin Hoffman/Muller Brockman school of thought, let alone of Weingart's. Nor acolytes of the New York school typified by Dorfsman/Rand/Lubalin. His background was hands-on grafting in good workaday studios. A school of hard knocks rather than a forum of fancy philosophies.

I'm making this point as Michael's work doesn't reflect an ideological stance or pronounced personal attitude. Nothing wrong with that, but, at least in my opinion, it positions him as more of a pragmatic art director than an obsessive designer, more broad brushstroke than meticulous dovetail. This is not

comme un danger public... Cette facette de sa personnalité doit s'expliquer autrement.

En décidant de faire carrière seul, ou plus précisément avec un partenaire d'une extrême discrétion nommé Banks – Michael aurait pu se suffire à lui-même mais il a toujours eu tendance à en faire trop – il entame le parcours qu'on lui connaît. Banks a quitté le monde du design voici quelques années, faisant ainsi de l'agence johnson banks, installée dans un coin perdu plein de charme du Clapham Common (une banlieue rurale de Londres, au sud de la Tamise), le laboratoire du seul Johnson. Situé dans un spacieux hangar en brique de l'ère victorienne devenu un espace chaleureux, on y entend le bruit des feuilles contre les carreaux et la rumeur des voitures au loin. L'équipe, de moins d'une dizaine de personnes, travaille avec acharnement sous l'œil scrupuleux du patron. Après tout, comme l'a finement observé un ancien employé, « les clients achètent Michael Johnson », pas le travail du studio.

Michael est un individu intelligent, charmant, sensible, ambitieux... et il a du succès. Derrière l'enthousiasme qu'on lui connaît se cache une intelligence affûtée comme une mine de crayon 6H. Il aime à discourir et sait manier le verbe. Il est convaincu que un et un doivent faire trois, manipule volontiers les idées et les concepts, évite (et dédaigne) les lubies et les modes graphiques. En d'autres termes, il est son propre souverain.

to say the work has no style. It does. But of arm-length-orchestration rather than piccolo playing. No "loose cannon" characteristics here, rather the opposite in fact, so the reason must lie elsewhere.

The decision to go solo – or at least along with a silent partner called Banks; Michael has a tendency to exaggerate; one would have been adequate – set him on his current trajectory. Banks left the scene after a couple of years so today johnson banks is Michael Johnson. Work takes place in a charming backwater in rural Clapham Common. A district of London south of the river. A Victorian shed with an agreeably converted spacious interior, bare brickwork, leaves tapping on the window panes, and the distant hum of traffic. The team, half a dozen or more, are hard at work under his scrupulous eye. After all, as a former employee has astutely observed, "the clients buy Michael Johnson", not the studio.

As an individual Michael is intelligent, charming, perceptive and ambitious. And successful. Beneath his casual enthusiasms he's as sharp as a 6H pencil. He is into discourse and has a neat way with words. He knows that one plus one are best calculated to produce three, readily deals in ideas and concepts, and avoids (as well as disdains) graphic fads and fashions. In other words he is his own man.

On peut aussi dire qu'il est ou semble être assez ingénu, voire naïf, et qu'il croit beaucoup à ce qu'il fait, qu'il tient à le partager. Cette association de naïveté et de générosité peut le mettre en péril lorsqu'il doit faire face à l'incompréhension des gens auxquels il a affaire. C'est là un habile stratagème, quoique inconscient, puisqu'il fait porter la responsabilité de l'équivoque à chacun de ses interlocuteurs. Michael n'est là que pour tourner la manivelle de l'orgue de barbarie. Qui sait si vous finirez singe, orgue ou badaud.

J'ai un jour reçu une carte de vœux de sa part, une photo de famille. Ce cliché m'a ouvert les yeux : je ne l'avais jamais imaginé en père, mais pourtant toute une famille était là, sur la photo. On reconnaît bien Michael, l'air sérieux, lunettes à monture de corne, cheveux brun-roux. J'ai appelé des collègues londoniens pour leur demander s'ils avaient déjà rencontré la femme de Michael, ou un de ses deux enfants. Réponse unanime : non. Conclusion : Michael mène une double vie. L'une, publique, consiste en une intense activité de designer en studio. L'autre commence au retour du bureau, à la maison. Ici, j'écris donc au sujet d'un quart d'homme. Au sujet de quelqu'un qui, pour autant que je sache, n'a encore rien révélé de la deuxième moitié de son existence (il a eu 40 ans en 2004) et qui dissimule habilement la moitié domestique de la première ère de sa vie. Il y a vraiment quelque chose de troublant en lui.

He is also, or appears to be, rather ingenuous – naive even. A characteristic which, attached to a trusting nature, generates an impression that if you don't match and perform to his expectations, he will feel severely let down. This is a smart, if unconscious ploy, as responsibility for the quality of interaction is thrust upon whoever Michael happens to be talking with. In effect he becomes the organ grinder. Whether you end up as monkey, organ, or onlooker is anybody's guess.

He once sent me a Christmas card. A picture of the Johnson family. What an eye opener. I had never envisaged him as a family man but here they all were. You can pick out Michael, the one with the earnest expression, horn-rim glasses and auburn locks. I called some fellow designers around town. "Have you ever met Michael's wife," I asked, "Or either of his two children?" No one had. Conclusion: Michael leads a double life. One of intense public design activity at the studio and another life back home. So here I am writing about a quarter man. Someone who, as far as I'm aware, hasn't revealed anything about the first half of his life (he was 40 in 2004) and keeps the domestic half of his second era similarly under wraps. There really is more to him than meets the eye.

Vous êtes peut-être en train de vous demander en quoi tout ce bavardage concerne le designer Michael Johnson. Comme je l'ai affirmé plus haut, je tiens à éclaircir sa façon d'envisager les choses. Lorsque j'ai affaire à une œuvre visuelle, j'ai tendance à ne pouvoir la dissocier de la personnalité de son créateur. Nous laissons toujours une trace de nous-mêmes dans les objets que nous produisons.

Le portfolio de son studio aligne les collaborations avec quelques valeurs sûres du milieu, ainsi qu'avec les institutions habituelles comme le Design Council, D&AD ou le British Council, et les forces vives du design que sont le Parc de la Villette, le Victoria and Albert Museum ou Phaidon, entre autres. Michael aime aussi œuvrer pour des causes nobles, donner de son temps. Il enseigne, fait des confé-rences, s'implique fréquemment dans des projets éducatifs. Il a récemment été élu président du club London's Design and Art Direction, une fonction aussi prenante que prestigieuse. On peut égale-ment préciser que sur ses étagères s'accumulent des trophées d'or et d'argent.

Plusieurs choses retiennent mon attention lorsque je passe en revue ses travaux. Les timbres inter-actifs réalisés pour le Royal Mail ont été un triomphe, non seulement parce que l'idée était brillante, mais aussi parce qu'il est effectivement parvenu à les faire produire – et c'est déterminant d'avoir réussi cela : l'expérience m'a appris que, si une bonne idée ne signifiait rien, le fait de la réaliser, en

Now you may wonder what all this chat has got to do with Michael Johnson the designer. As I stated up front I need to figure out how he goes about things. Well, it's a personal view, but when looking at graphic work I can't separate the personality of the creator from whatever it is they have created. We all leave a residue of ourselves in our products.

The studio portfolio has a roster of corporate blue chips, and the usual institutional suspects such as The Design Council, D&AD, The British Council, and design conscious bodies, Parc de la Villette, the V&A and Phaidon for example. Another aspect of Michael is his contribution to performing good works. He teaches and lectures. Is always willing to lend a helping hand to educational projects. Lately he was elected and served as President of London's 'Design and Art Direction' club. Indeed a time consuming as well as prestigious appointment. He also has a shedload of gold and silver awards.

Looking through his stuff I am struck by several things. The interactive stamps he designed for the Royal Mail are a triumph. Not only for the brilliant concept but because he actually managed to get them produced. Experience informs me that getting a good idea means dick, but getting it realised sep-

revanche, faisait vraiment la différence. Non content de trouver des solutions théoriques aux problèmes de création, Michael possède de toute évidence la ténacité qu'il faut pour leur donner une réalité.

J'aime sa transformation impromptue de la lettre H en une maison avec cheminée, pour l'organisation Shelter, qui a ouvert ce lieu aux sans-abri. J'aime aussi l'esprit dont il fait preuve en changeant un A en un signe « supérieur à », ou en choisissant le nouveau nom de la branche « assurance directe » d'une vénérable compagnie financière européenne. Michael n'excelle jamais autant que lorsqu'il doit opérer au sein d'une marge de manœuvre réduite. J'ai du respect pour ça, j'apprécie.

On ne s'étonnera pas de voir que les affiches qu'il réalise pour ses conférences semblent graphiquement plus libérées que le travail quotidien de son studio – qui doit forcément obéir à certaines contraintes –, ni de constater qu'il investit un temps et une énergie considérables pour les produire. On ne saurait douter de son goût du défi pour le défi.

Mais finalement, quel est le trait qui caractérise le mieux Michael Johnson ? Je dirais : son mode de pensée. Il est autant penseur qu'homme d'action. Il n'a pas de style ou de recette particulière, mais il a une pensée. Le texte qui suit est extrait d'un article écrit par Michael, intitulé « Quand le monde ziggue, zagguez ».

arates design sheep from design goats. In addition to solving creative problems Michael obviously has the tenacity and capacity to make them happen.

I like the off-the-cuff conversion of the letter h into a house with a chimney for Shelter. An organisation which provides just that for the homeless. And the wit of a "more than" sign in place of "A" in the logotype for "more than". The new name chosen for the direct insurance arm of a venerable European personal finance company. He has a sharp nose to exploit minimum opportunities. I empathise with that. It's no surprise that the posters he generates for his own lectures express considerably more graphic freedom than the day-to-day-constraint-ridden works produced by the studio. Nor that he invests so much thought and time into producing them. He obviously enjoys challenge for its own sake.

So what personal trait does Michael bring to the table? Well, I think it's thought. He's a thinker as well as a doer. He doesn't have a style or a formula, he has a thought. This is an extract from an article written by Michael entitled "when the world zigs, zag".

"I stole the headline", he declares, "from an old BBH poster for Levi's from the 80's which placed a black

« J'ai piqué le titre de cet article à une vieille affiche publicitaire Levi's des années 80. On y voyait un mouton noir au beau milieu d'un troupeau de moutons blancs, tous couverts de laine. Cette pub vous incitait à porter des jeans noirs, alors qu'à l'époque (1982), les jeans bleus étaient la norme. J'ai repris la phrase car les designers sont aussi des moutons : nous suivons les modes, que nous le voulions ou non. Quand on est un suiveur, on évite de se tromper ou d'être ridicule. En ce qui me concerne, je refuse de suivre ; je préfère aller dans le sens contraire de la marche. C'est ainsi que beaucoup de grandes idées ont vu le jour : en prenant le chemin contraire de celui qu'elles devaient suivre. Au lieu de zigguer comme les autres idées, elles ont zaggué. »
Nous y voici donc. Je vous l'avais dit : Michael est un danger public.

Alan Fletcher

sheep in the midst of a flock of white, fluffy ones. The ad dared you to wear black jeans at a time (1982) when, we can only presume, blue jeans ruled. I used it because graphic designers are sheep too, as we follow trends, whether we realise it or not. Thinking as a herd takes away the danger of doing something wrong, or doing something that might be ridiculed. But I don't believe in herd thinking – I like reverse thinking. Some of our best ideas have come from starting from precisely the opposite place to where we should be: zagging, when all around are zigging."
There you are. I said he was a loose cannon.

Alan Fletcher

small   sma

Comparative superlative

Comparative: add -er to compare two objects.
Superlative: add -est when more than two objects.

UK or USA A word which has different and sometimes opposite meanings in the UK and USA. For example 'jelly' is a dessert in the UK and a preserve in the USA

● ● BRITISH
● ● COUNCIL

drink drank drunk

Irregular verbs The present, past participle and past describing the process and the finished state

● ● BRITISH
● ● COUNCIL

14

AFFICHES POUR LES
CLASSES DU
BRITISH COUNCIL
62 x 28,5 CM
LITHOGRAPHIE EN
QUADRICHROMIE
GRANDE-BRETAGNE
1998, MODIFIÉES
EN 2004

BRITISH COUNCIL
CLASSROOM CARDS
BRITISH COUNCIL
62 x 28.5 CM
4 COLOUR LITHO
PRINTING
UK
1998, REDESIGNED
2004

Homophones Words which have the same sound but a different spelling and meaning.

BRITISH COUNCIL

Cockney rhyming slang Slang, originating in the East End of London. A word is replaced by rhyming words or phrases.

BRITISH COUNCIL

Shelter

home
hope
here
share
change
sheltered
wish
children

One million children in Britain suffer in bad housing.

Over a million children in Britain live in bad housing.

Bad housing wrecks lives

Shelter

Joe Barrell
Head of Publishing & Editorial

Publishing & Editorial
88 Old Street
London
EC1V 9HU
t 020 7505 2044
f 020 7505 2030
joe_barrell@shelter.org.uk
www.shelter.org.uk

One million children in Britain suffer in bad housing.

Bad housing wrecks lives

Shelter

Bad housing wrecks lives

Bad housing wrecks lives

IDENTITÉ VISUELLE
SHELTER, ASSOCIATION D'AIDE AU LOGEMENT
DIFFÉRENTS FORMATS
DÉCALCOMANIE, LITHOGRAPHIE,
FLEXOGRAPHIE
GRANDE-BRETAGNE
2004

CORPORATE IDENTITY
SHELTER HOUSING CHARITY
VARIOUS FORMATS
DECALS, LITHO PRINTING, FLEXOGRAPHY
UK
2004

BROCHURE
SMURFIT TOWNSEND HOOK
A4
LITHOGRAPHIE EN QUADRICHROMIE
GRANDE-BRETAGNE
2001

FAB PAPER BROCHURE
SMURFIT TOWNSEND HOOK
A4
4 COLOUR LITHO PRINTING
UK
2001

INVITATION POUR LE DÎNER DA WO
DESIGN COUNCIL
45 MOTS MAGNÉTIQUES, 21 x 9.9 CM
SÉRIGRAPHIE
GRANDE-BRETAGNE
1994

DA WO DINNER INVITE
DESIGN COUNCIL
45 MAGNETIC WORDS, 21 x 9.9 CM
SCREENPRINTING
UK
1994

[PANTALON COMPTANT]
CREATION GALLERY, GINZA
JEAN BLANC
IMPRESSION NUMÉRIQUE
JAPON
2005

COUNTING TROUSERS
CREATION GALLERY, GINZA
WHITE JEANS
DIGITAL PRINTING
JAPAN
2005

23

AFFICHES POUR
LE BRITISH COUNCIL
A1
LITHOGRAPHIE EN QUADRICHROMIE
GRANDE-BRETAGNE
1998

BRITISH COUNCIL
CORRIDOR POSTERS
A1
4 COLOUR LITHO PRINTING
UK
1998

BRITAIN

Comedians

Benny Hill
The comedian became famed worldwide for his ribald, seaside humour, Hill's Angels and such characters as Fred Scuttle, Maurice Dribble, The Halitosis Kid and Barney the Disgruntled Husband.

Rowan Atkinson
The rubber faced star best known for the accident prone Mr Bean and the unlikeable Blackadder. Films include 'Four Weddings And A Funeral', 'Bean – The Movie' and the voice of Zazu in 'The Lion King'.

The British Council

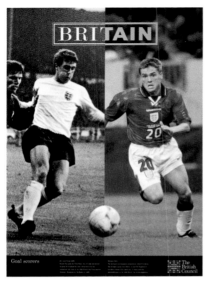

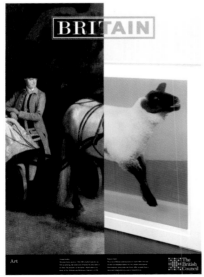

**Art Center College Library
1700 Lida Street
Pasadena, CA 91103**

IDENTITÉ VISUELLE
VICTORIA AND ALBERT MUSEUM
PHOTOGRAPHIES RETOUCHÉES
NUMÉRIQUEMENT
GRANDE-BRETAGNE
2001

BRITISH GALLERIES CORPORATE IDENTITY
VICTORIA AND ALBERT MUSEUM
DIGITALLY RETOUCHED PHOTOGRAPHIC
IMAGES
UK
2001

IDENTITÉ VISUELLE
AGENCE DE RECRUTEMENT CANNA KENDALL
PAPETERIE (A4, A5), CARTES DE VISITE
LITHOGRAPHIE EN QUADRICHROMIE
GRANDE-BRETAGNE
1996

CORPORATE IDENTITY
CANNA KENDALL RECRUITMENT AGENCY
STATIONERY (A4, A5), BUSINESS CARDS
4 COLOUR LITHO PRINTING
UK
1996

Design

U | **Charles Rennie Mackintosh**
Architect, designer and artist (1868–1928). Mackintosh blended Scottish traditions with Art Nouveau and Japanese forms. Most famous for tea room interiors, private houses and the Glasgow School of Art (known as the Mackintosh Building).

K | **iMac**
The revolutionary iMac was Apple's computer for the new millennium. Created in 1998 by British designer Jonathan Ive with the Internet in mind. The most innovative computer since the original 1984 Mac, with stylish translucent coloured plastics.

$$\frac{U}{K}$$

The British Council

Information
U
K
U K
The World Wide Web Consortium
The British Council

Moving image
U
K
U
K
The British Council

Looking at **light**

Take an area. **Where is the light?** What kind of light is used? **Is the light natural or artificial, bright or dull?** Can the lighting change to suit different times of day or different seasons? **Is the light right for different activities?** Are there any problems?

Design Council

Looking at **signs**

Find and explain a sign. **What does the sign tell you?** Does it tell you where to go, how to behave or where to find something? **Does it use colour, symbols, pictograms or words?** Is it clear? **Who is the sign for?** How do we know? **Where is it?** Is it easy to see? **Is it part of a sign system?**

Design Council

Looking at **safety**

Look carefully around one area. **Is there something you think could be dangerous?** Is there anything that warns you of the danger? **Describe the danger.** Is it likely an accident could happen? **Who might be at risk?** How could you make it safe?

Design Council

[LES ENJEUX DU DESIGN, AFFICHES PÉDAGOGIQUES]
DESIGN COUNCIL
A1
LITHOGRAPHIE EN QUADRICHROMIE
GRANDE-BRETAGNE
1996

DESIGN DECISIONS TEACHERS POSTERS
DESIGN COUNCIL
A1
4 COLOUR LITHO PRINTING
UK
1996

RAPPORT ANNUEL
DESIGN COUNCIL
A4
LITHOGRAPHIE EN BICHROMIE
ET QUADRICHROMIE
GRANDE-BRETAGNE
2001

ANNUAL REVIEW
DESIGN COUNCIL
A4
2/4 COLOUR LITHO PRINTING
UK
2001

NAPPIES TAKE

species ref.3644 596   102

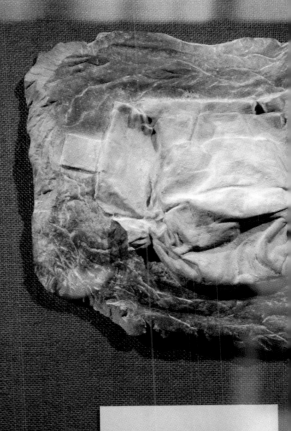

CENTURIES TO

species ref.3644 123   103

DECOMPOSE

species ref.3644 941   104

MICHAEL JOHNSON,
JOHNSON BANKS,
CRESENT WORKS,
CRESENT LANE,
CLAPHAM,
LONDON SW4 9RW

Royal Mail   Tyneside   Mail
27.03.03
2003

MICHAEL JOHNSON,
JOHNSON BANKS,
CRESENT WORKS,
CRESENT LANE,
CLAPHAM,
LONDON SW4 9RW.

[TIMBRES FRUITS ET LÉGUMES]
ROYAL MAIL
10 TIMBRES ET 76 AUTOCOLLANTS
DÉCOUPÉS À L'EMPORTE-PIÈCE
PHOTO-GRAVURE
GRANDE-BRETAGNE
2003

FRUIT AND VEG STAMPS
ROYAL MAIL
10 DIE-CUT STAMPS,
76 DIE-CUT STICKERS
PHOTO-GRAVURE
UK
2003

40

VISUEL DE L'EXPOSITION
« WILLIAM MORRIS »
VICTORIA AND ALBERT
MUSEUM
PHOTOGRAPHIE
GRANDE-BRETAGNE
1996

"WILLIAM MORRIS" EXHIBITION
SYMBOL
VICTORIA AND ALBERT MUSEUM
PHOTOGRAPH
UK
1996

A COMPREHENSIVE
GUIDE TO THE BEST
GARDEN SHOPS SELLING
AND IN THE UK
INCLUDING INTERVIEWS
WITH TOP GARDEN
DESIGNERS WOULD BE
BLOOMING HANDY

ROB CASSY

GARDEN UK

ROB CASSY

COUVERTURE DU LIVRE
GARDEN UK
CONRAN OCTOPUS
14,8 x 16,2 CM
SÉRIGRAPHIE
GRANDE-BRETAGNE
2003

GARDEN UK BOOK COVER
CONRAN OCTOPUS
14,8 x 16,2 CM
SCREENPRINTING
UK
2003

designerguißisap / 036 / JOHNSON BANKS

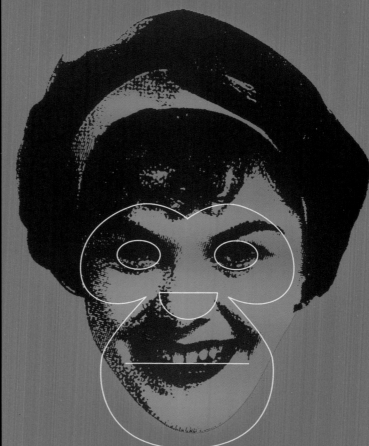
chimps in wigs

an exhibition of new work by david s'higgins at the arts theatre café 6/7 great newport street london wc'h 7jh exhibition runs until 31st december

AFFICHE DE L'EXPOSITION
« CHIMPS IN WIGS »
DAVID O'HIGGINS
A1
LITHOGRAPHIE EN QUADRICHROMIE
GRANDE-BRETAGNE, 1994

"CHIMPS IN WIGS"
EXHIBITION POSTER
DAVID O'HIGGINS
A1
4 COLOUR LITHO
UK, 1994

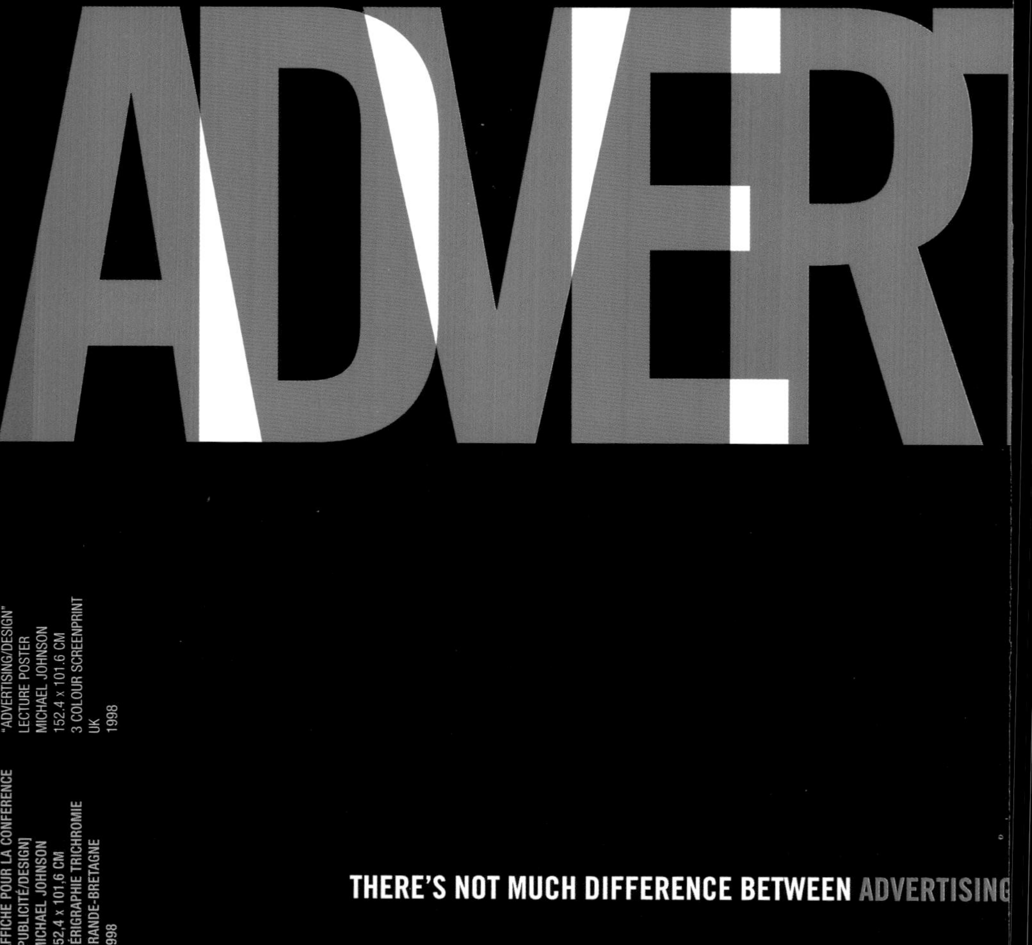

ADVERT

THERE'S NOT MUCH DIFFERENCE BETWEEN ADVERTISING

DESIGN A TALK BY MICHAEL JOHNSON JOHNSON BANKS

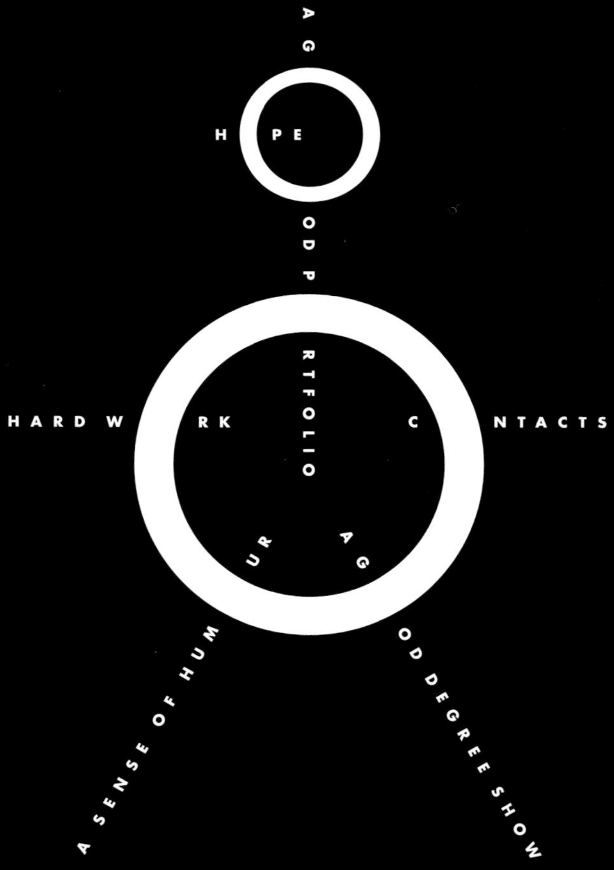

A GOOD PORTFOLIO
HOPE
A GOOD DEGREE SHOW
HARD WORK
CONTACTS
A SENSE OF HUMOUR

AFFICHE POUR LA CONFÉRENCE
[L'ÉTUDIANT PARFAIT]
MICHAEL JOHNSON
152,4 x 101,6 CM
LITHOGRAPHIE MONOCHROME
GRANDE-BRETAGNE
2000

"PERFECT STUDENT"
LECTURE POSTER
MICHAEL JOHNSON
152,4 x 101,6 CM
1 COLOUR SCREENPRINT
UK
2000

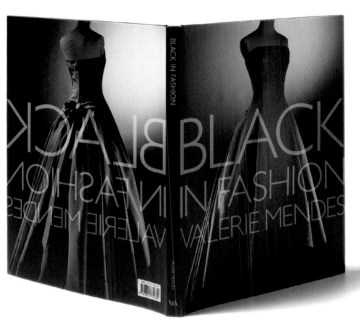

BLACK IN FASHION BOOK COVER
V&A PUBLISHING
A3
4 COLOUR LITHO PRINTING
2000

COUVERTURE DU LIVRE *BLACK IN FASHION*
V&A PUBLISHING
A3
LITHOGRAPHIE EN QUADRICHROMIE
GRANDE-BRETAGNE
2000

DESIGN UK / FASHION UK
CONRAN OCTOPUS
14.8 x 16.2 CM
EMBOSSED RUBBER, MACHINE
EMBROIDERED CLOTH
UK
1999/2001

DESIGN UK / FASHION UK
CONRAN OCTOPUS
14,8 x 16,2 CM
CAOUTCHOUC GAUFRÉ,
TOILE BRODÉE À LA MACHINE
GRANDE-BRETAGNE
1999/2001

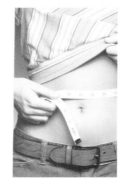

KUSHTI Kushti KUSHTI

IDENTITÉ VISUELLE
SOCIÉTÉ DE CONSEIL KUSHTI
PAPETERIE
LITHOGRAPHIE EN QUADRICHROMIE
GRANDE-BRETAGNE
2002

CORPORATE IDENTITY
KUSHTI CONSULTING
STATIONERY
4 COLOUR LITHO PRINTING
UK
2002

PARC LA VILLETTE

PAGE PRÉCÉDENTE :
IDENTITÉ VISUELLE
PARC DE LA VILLETTE
LOGO
LITHOGRAPHIE EN
QUADRICHROMIE
FRANCE
1999

PREVIOUS PAGE:
CORPORATE IDENTITY
PARC DE LA VILLETTE
LOGO
4 COLOUR LITHO PRINTING
FRANCE
1999

[CHAISE-LONGUE GAZON]
PARC DE LA VILLETTE
PHOTOGRAPHIE RETOUCHÉE
FRANCE
2001/2002

GRASS DECKCHAIR
PARC DE LA VILLETTE
RETOUCHED PHOTOGRAPHY
FRANCE
2001/2002

GAUCHE :
PUBLICITÉ POUR LE CINÉMA
PARC DE LA VILLETTE
FILM 35 MM
FRANCE
2000/2001

DROITE :
[PANTALON GAZON]
PARC DE LA VILLETTE
PHOTOGRAPHIE RETOUCHÉE
FRANCE
2001/2002

LEFT:
CINEMA COMMERCIAL
PARC DE LA VILLETTE
35 MM FILM
FRANCE
2000/2001

RIGHT:
GRASS TROUSERS
PARC DE LA VILLETTE
RETOUCHED PHOTOGRAPHY
FRANCE
2001/2002

AFFICHE « BYE BYE PROSPERO »
POUR LE CNAC
PARC DE LA VILLETTE
120 x 176 CM
LITHOGRAPHIE EN QUADRICHROMIE
FRANCE
2003

CNAC "BYE BYE PROSPERO"
POSTER
PARC DE LA VILLETTE
120 x 176 CM
4 COLOUR LITHO
FRANCE
2003

AFFICHE DE L'EXPOSITION « MALI-KOW »
PARC DE LA VILLETTE
120 x 176 CM
LITHOGRAPHIE EN QUADRICHROMIE
FRANCE
2001

"MALI-KOW" EXHIBITION POSTER
PARC DE LA VILLETTE
120 x 176 CM
4 COLOUR LITHO
FRANCE
2001

AFFICHE DE L'EXPOSITION « INDIENS »
PARC DE LA VILLETTE
120 x 176 CM
LITHOGRAPHIE EN QUADRICHROMIE
FRANCE
2002

"INDIENS" EXHIBITION POSTER
PARC DE LA VILLETTE
120 x 176 CM
4 COLOUR LITHO PRINTING
FRANCE
2002

AFFICHE DE « MACBETH »
PARC DE LA VILLETTE
120 x 176 CM
LITHOGRAPHIE EN QUADRICHROMIE
FRANCE
2002

"MACBETH" POSTER
PARC DE LA VILLETTE
120 x 176 CM
4 COLOUR LITHO
FRANCE
2002

BIENNALE INTERNATIONALE DES ARTS DE LA
MARIONNETTE

30 MAI - 3 JUIN PARC LA VILLETTE > M PORTE DE PANTIN
8/9/10 JUIN FERME DU BUISSON > RER A - NOISIEL
AVEC LE THÉÂTRE DE LA MARIONNETTE À PARIS
INFO / RÉSA 01 40 03 75 75 / 01 64 62 77 77   WWW.THEATREDELAMARIONNETTE.COM

MARIONETTE BIENNALE POSTER
PARC DE LA VILLETTE
120 x 176 CM
4 COLOUR LITHO
FRANCE
2001

AFFICHE POUR LA BIENNALE
DES ARTS DE LA MARIONNETTE
PARC DE LA VILLETTE
120 x 176 CM
LITHOGRAPHIE EN QUADRICHROMIE
FRANCE
2001

designerqujšsap / 036 / JOHNSON BANKS

The First World War Remembered

An exhibition
commemorating
the eightieth
anniversary
of the end of the
First World War.
18 September –
28 December 1998
Imperial War Museum
⊖ Lambeth North or
Elephant and Castle
For exhibition
information
and details
of associated
special events
tel 0171 416 5000
www.iwm.org.uk

LOGO
SOCIÉTÉ FINANCIÈRE D'INNOVATION
FORESIGHT
GRANDE-BRETAGNE
2004

LOGO
FORESIGHT VENTURE CAPITAL
UK
2004

IDENTITÉ VISUELLE POUR ECCA
ORGANISME D'AIDE AUX JEUNES
ENTREPRENEURS DANS LE DOMAINE
DE LA CRÉATION
PAPETERIE, CARTES POSTALES
LITHOGRAPHIE EN QUADRICHROMIE
GRANDE-BRETAGNE
2004

ECCA CORPORATE IDENTITY
ENTERPRISE CENTRE FOR THE CREATIVE ARTS
STATIONERY, POSTCARDS
4 COLOUR LITHO
UK
2004

ECCA
Enterprise
Centre
for the
Creative
Arts

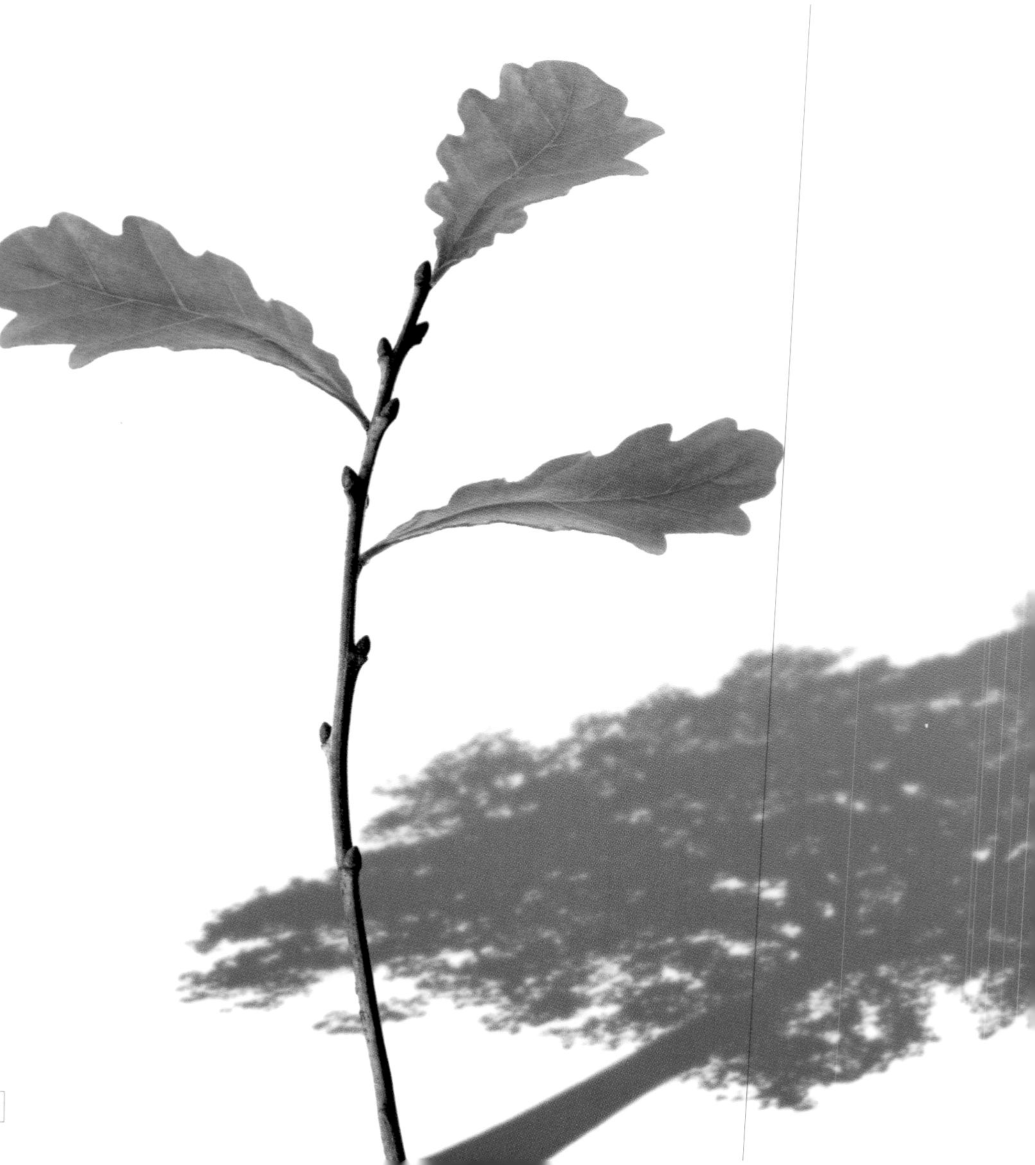

IDENTITÉ VISUELLE DE LA CAMPAGNE
D'AFFICHAGE [CONSTRUIRE POUR LE FUTUR]
GOUVERNEMENT BRITANNIQUE
SÉRIGRAPHIE EN QUADRICHROMIE,
DÉCALCOMANIE
GRANDE-BRETAGNE
1997/1998

BUILDING FOR THE FUTURE IDENTITY
HM GOVERNMENT
BUILDING SITE SIGNAGE
4 COLOUR SCREENPRINTING,
DECALS
UK
1997/1998

IDENTITÉ VISUELLE
ASSURANCE DIRECTE MORE TH>N
FORMATS ET TECHNIQUES DIVERS
GRANDE-BRETAGNE
2001

IDENTITY
MORE TH>N DIRECT INSURANCE
VARIOUS FORMATS
VARIOUS TECHNIQUES
UK
2001

designergu&sap / 036 / JOHNSON BANKS

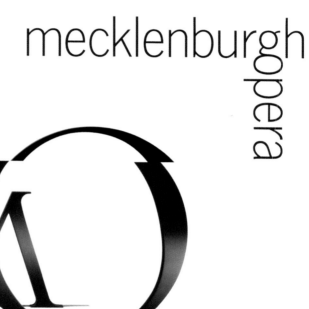

mecklenburgh opera

IDENTITÉ VISUELLE
OPÉRA DE MECKLENBURGH
LOGO, AFFICHE A1
LITHOGRAPHIE EN
QUADRICHROMIE
GRANDE-BRETAGNE
1996

IDENTITY
MECKLENBURGH OPERA
LOGO, POSTER A1
4 COLOUR LITHO
UK
1996

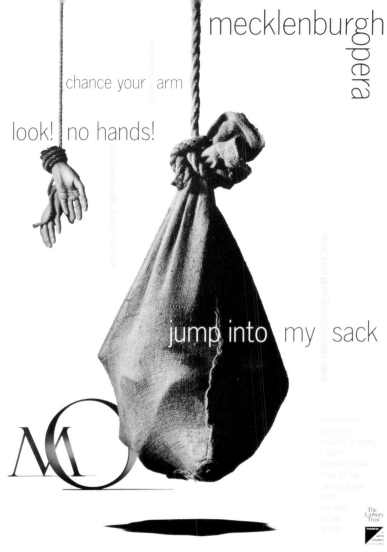

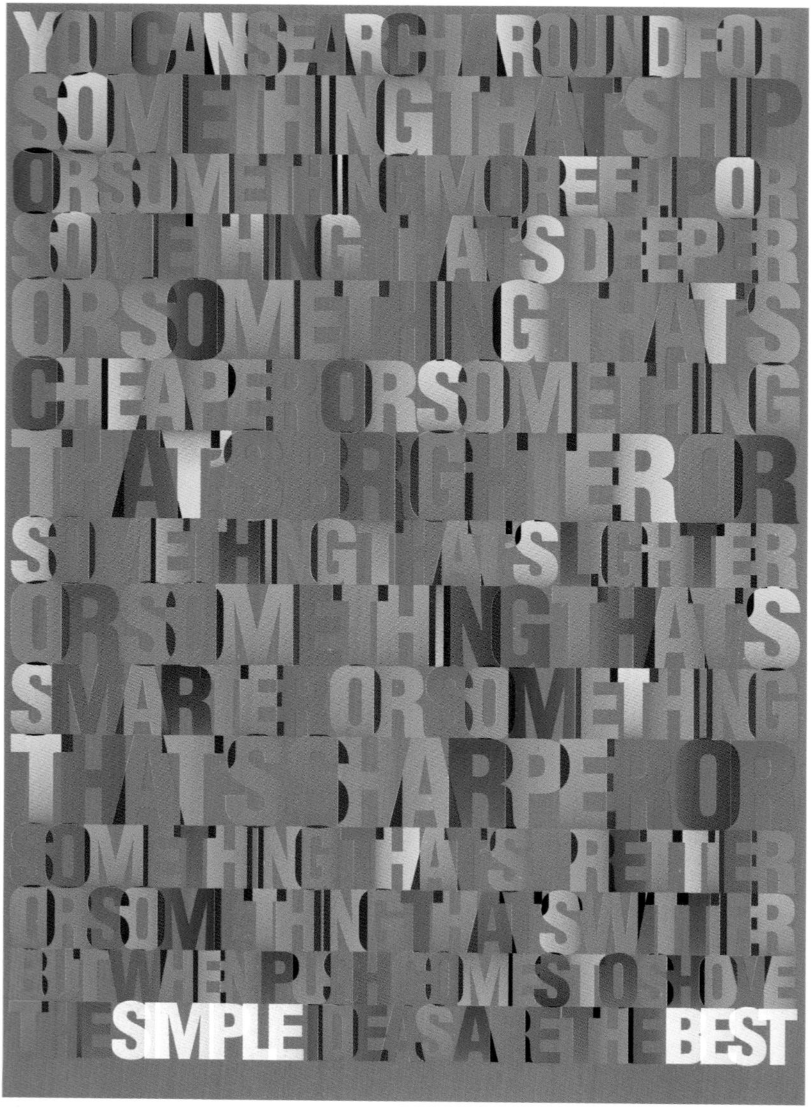

AFFICHE [LES IDÉES SIMPLES
SONT LES MEILLEURES]
MICHAEL JOHNSON
152,4 CM x 101,6 CM
LITHOGRAPHIE EN QUADRICHROMIE
GRANDE-BRETAGNE
1997

"SIMPLE IDEAS ARE THE BEST"
POSTER
MICHAEL JOHNSON
152,4 x 101,6 CM
4 COLOUR LITHO
UK
1997

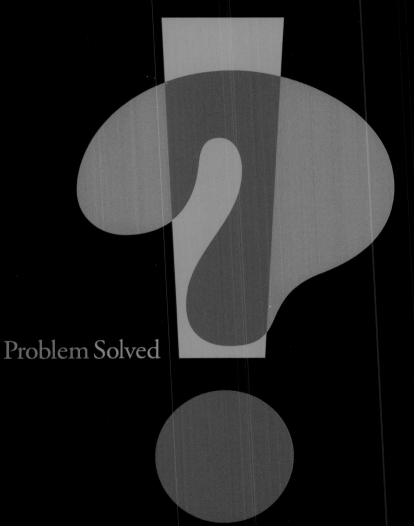

Problem Solved

VISUEL DU LIVRE *PROBLEM SOLVED*   *PROBLEM SOLVED* BOOK SYMBOL
PHAIDON PRESS   PHAIDON PRESS
COUVERTURE DE LIVRE   BOOK COVER
LITHOGRAPHIE EN QUADRICHROMIE   4 COLOUR LITHO
GRANDE-BRETAGNE   UK
2002   2002

designergud:sap / 036 / JOHNSON BANKS

D&AD (DESIGN AND ART
DIRECTION) COUVERTURE
DU NUMÉRO ANNUEL
20 x 28,5 CM
CAOUTCHOUC JAUNE GAUFRÉ
À FROID, TOILE, FERMETURE
ÉCLAIR
GRANDE-BRETAGNE
1994

D&AD (DESIGN AND ART
DIRECTION) ANNUAL COVER
20 x 28,5 CM
BLIND EMBOSSED YELLOW
RUBBER, CLOTH, ZIPPER
UK
1994

1998 D&AD GOLD AWARD
FOR THE MOST OUTSTANDING _____

APPEL À CONTRIBUTION DE *D&AD*
A4
LITHOGRAPHIE EN
QUADRICHROMIE
GRANDE-BRETAGNE
1997

D&AD CALL FOR ENTRIES
A4
4 COLOUR LITHO
UK
1997

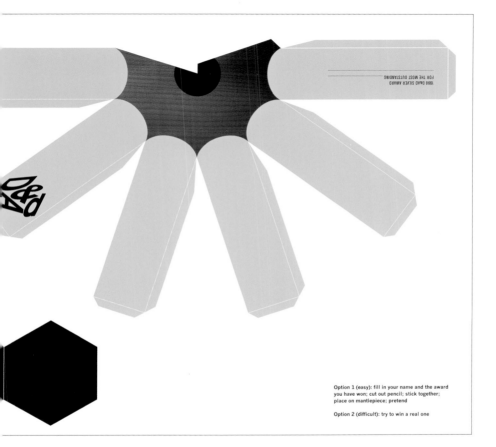

Option 1 (easy): fill in your name and the award
you have won; cut out pencil; stick together;
place on mantlepiece; pretend

Option 2 (difficult): try to win a real one

VISUEL DE L'EXPOSITION « REWIND »
D&AD
GRANDE-BRETAGNE
2002

"REWIND" EXHIBITION SYMBOL
D&AD
UK
2002

AFFICHES REWIND + SIGNALÉTIQUE
DE L'EXPOSITION
DESIGN AND ART DIRECTION
AFFICHES 50,8 x 86,2 CM,
PANNEAUX D'EXPOSITION
LITHOGRAPHIE EN QUADRICHROMIE,
IMPRESSION NUMÉRIQUE
GRANDE-BRETAGNE
2002

REWIND POSTERS + EXHIBITION
DESIGN AND ART DIRECTION
50,8 x 86,2 CM POSTERS,
EXHIBITION PANELS
4 COLOUR LITHO,
DIGITAL OUTPUTS
UK
2002

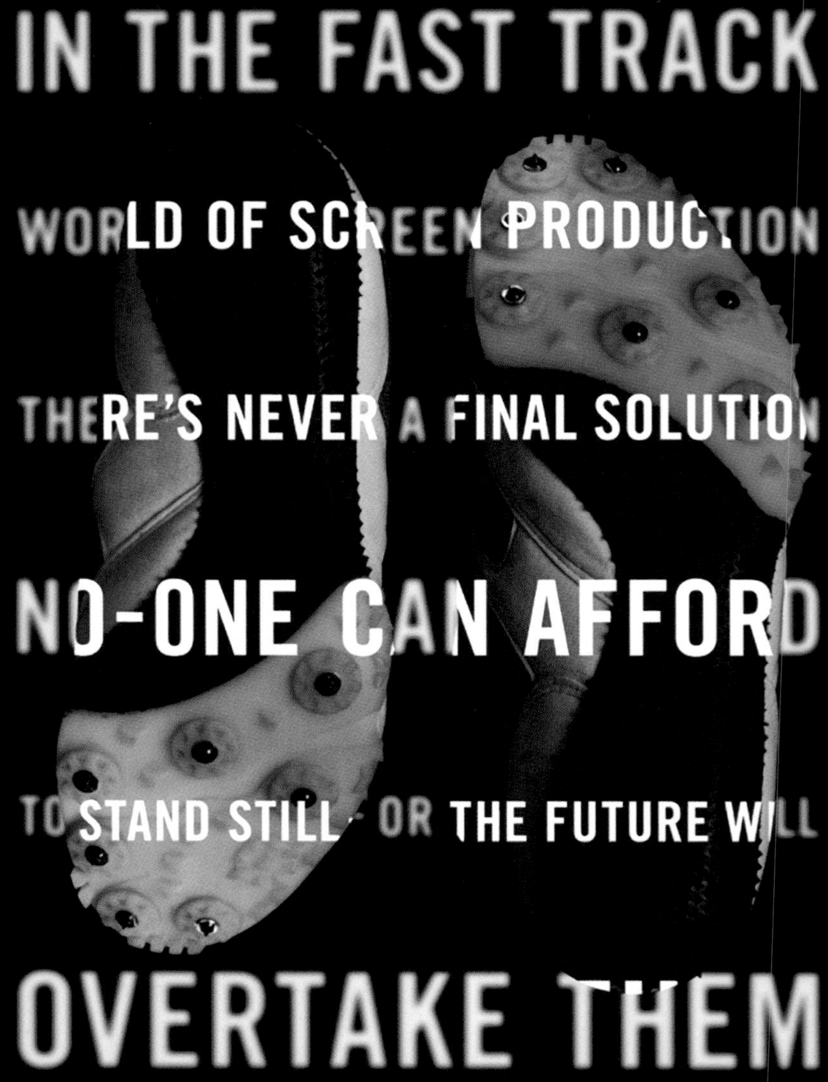

IN THE FAST TRACK

WORLD OF SCREEN PRODUCTION

THERE'S NEVER A FINAL SOLUTION

NO-ONE CAN AFFORD

TO STAND STILL · OR THE FUTURE WILL

OVERTAKE THEM

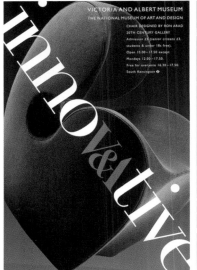

WONDERBRA BY PLAYTEX
DRESS COLLECTION
Admission £5 (senior citizens £3,
students & under 18s free).
Open 10.00 – 17.50 except
Mondays 12.00 – 17.50.
Free for everyone 16.30 – 17.50.
South Kensington ⊖

VICTORIA AND ALBERT MUSEUM
THE NATIONAL MUSEUM OF ART AND DESIGN

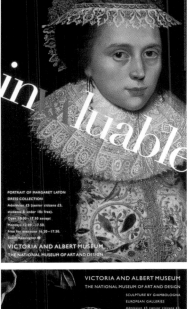

PORTRAIT OF MARGARET LATON
DRESS COLLECTION
Admission £5 (senior citizens £3,
students & under 18s free).
Open 10.00 – 17.50 except
Mondays 12.00 – 17.50.
Free for everyone 16.30 – 17.50.
South Kensington ⊖

VICTORIA AND ALBERT MUSEUM
THE NATIONAL MUSEUM OF ART AND DESIGN

VICTORIA AND ALBERT MUSEUM
THE NATIONAL MUSEUM OF ART AND DESIGN
CHAIR DESIGNED BY RON ARAD
20TH CENTURY GALLERY
Admission £5 (senior citizens £3,
students & under 18s free).
Open 10.00 – 17.50 except
Mondays 12.00 – 17.50.
Free for everyone 16.30 – 17.50.
South Kensington ⊖

VICTORIA AND ALBERT MUSEUM
THE NATIONAL MUSEUM OF ART AND DESIGN
SCULPTURE BY GIAMBOLOGNA
EUROPEAN GALLERIES
Admission £5 (senior citizens £3,
students & under 18s free).
Open 10.00 – 17.50 except
Mondays 12.00 – 17.50.
Free for everyone 16.30 – 17.50
South Kensington ⊖

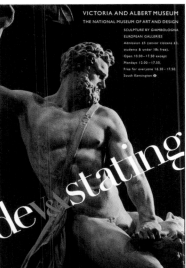

SUMMER POSTERS
VICTORIA AND ALBERT MUSEUM
152.4 x 101.6 CM
4 COLOUR LITHO
UK
1997

AFFICHES SAISONNIÈRES
VICTORIA AND ALBERT MUSEUM
152.4 x 101.6 CM
LITHOGRAPHIE EN QUADRICHROMIE
GRANDE-BRETAGNE
1997

PAGE 76 :
NATIONAL FILM AND
TELEVISION SCHOOL
ANNUAL REPORT
A4
4 COLOUR LITHO
UK
1994

PAGE 76 :
RAPPORT ANNUEL
NATIONAL SCHOOL OF FILM
AND TELEVISION
A4
LITHOGRAPHIE EN QUADRICHROMIE
GRANDE-BRETAGNE
1994

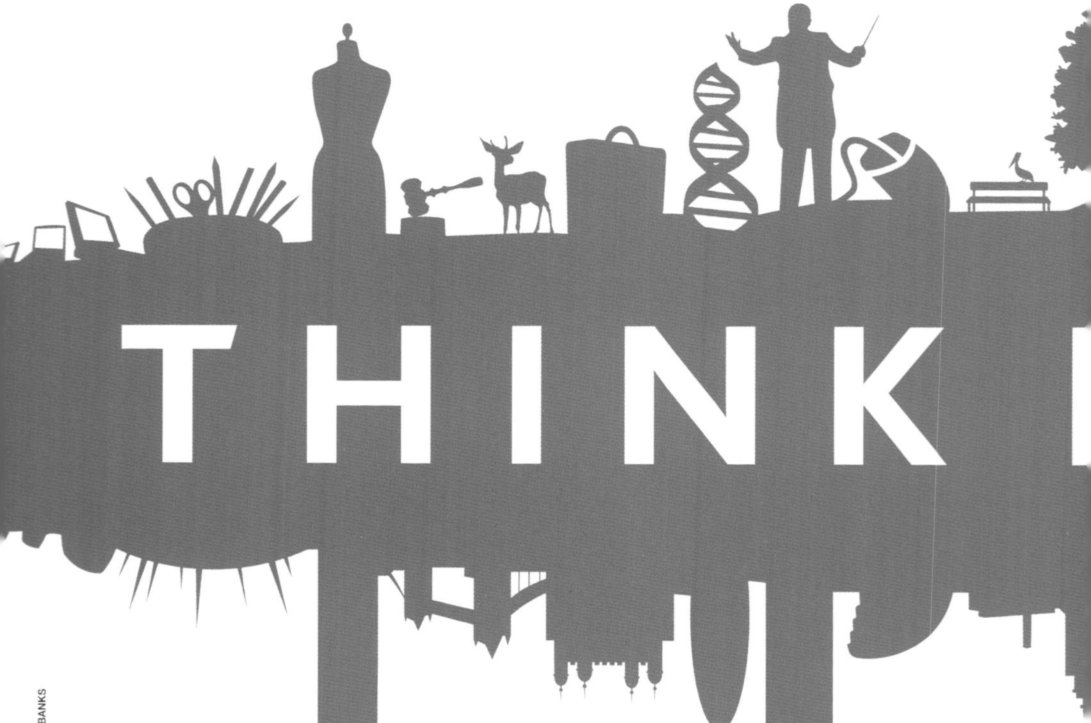
THINK

LOGO
THINK LONDON
GRANDE-BRETAGNE
2004

LOGO
THINK LONDON
UK
2004

designer/ຊ່ງຊ່sap / 036 / JOHNSON BANKS

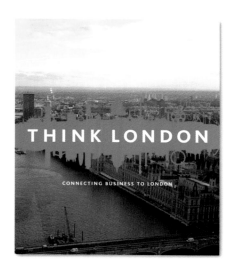

APPLICATIONS DE
L'IDENTITÉ VISUELLE
THINK LONDON
A4, BROCHURE
ACCORDÉON A6,
BANNIÈRES
INTERNET
LITHOGRAPHIE
EN BICHROMIE
ET QUADRICHROMIE
GRANDE-BRETAGNE
2004

IDENTITY
APPLICATIONS
THINK LONDON
A4, A6 CONCERTINA,
WEB HEADERS
2/4 COLOUR LITHO
UK
2004

THE REVOLUTION
IS COMING
MARCH 3RD 2004

FREEDOM
FOR
LONDON

AFFICHES LONDON REPUBLIK
TIME OUT
A1
LITHOGRAPHIE EN QUADRICHROMIE
GRANDE-BRETAGNE
2004

LONDON REPUBLIK POSTERS
TIME OUT
A1
4 COLOUR LITHO
UK
2004

the spiral

BROCHURE PROMOTIONNELLE
VICTORIA AND ALBERT MUSEUM
BOÎTE DE 20 x 22,5 x 16 CM
LITHOGRAPHIE EN BICHROMIE +
EMPORTE-PIÈCE
GRANDE-BRETAGNE
1998

SPIRAL MAILER
VICTORIA AND ALBERT MUSEUM
20 x 22.5 x 16 CM BOX
2 COLOUR LITHO + DIE-CUTTING
UK
1998

[SIGNALISATION DU HALL
D'ACCUEIL]
SCIENCE MUSEUM
PANNEAUX LUMINEUX
2 x 4 M, LETTRES DE NÉON
CLIGNOTANTES
GRANDE-BRETAGNE
2001

WELCOME WING SIGNAGE
SCIENCE MUSEUM
2 x 4 M ILLUMINATED SIGNS,
INTERNALLY LIT LIGHT-BOXES
WITH PULSING NEON LETTERS
UK
2001

LONDON SOUTH 01/02   www.yell.com

NURSERY SCHOOLS

LONDON SOUTH 00/01   www.yell.com

YELLOW PAGES

SWIMMING INSTRUCTORS

ES

www.yell.co.uk

YELLOW PAGES

The brief: design a new typeface for the Yellow Pages
Directory which allows more characters per line,
is cleaner and more readable at very small sizes and
can be used with negative leading.

Ascenders
75% of
normal height

Bottom of counter
amended to allow
for ink fill

Condensed basic form

abcdefg

Junctions chiselled
away to allow for
fill in at very small
type sizes

Bottom stroke
thinned to allow
for ink spread

Descenders
75% of
normal height

COUVERTURES
PAGES JAUNES BRITANNIQUES
A4
LITHOGRAPHIE 5 COULEURS
GRANDE-BRETAGNE
1998/2003

COVERS
YELLOW PAGES
A4
5 COLOUR LITHO
UK
1998/2003

CRÉATION D'UNE POLICE
DE CARACTÈRES POUR LES PAGES
JAUNES BRITANNIQUES
GRANDE-BRETAGNE
1998

TYPEFACE
YELLOW PAGES
UK
1998

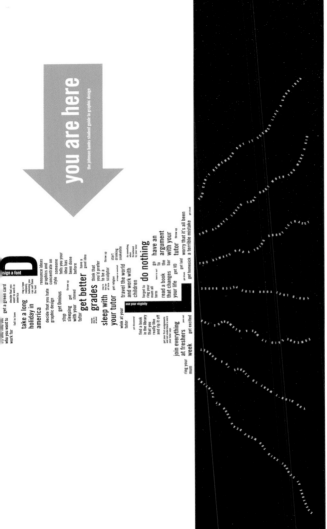

AFFICHE [VOUS ÊTES ICI]
MICHAEL JOHNSON
147.3 x 101.6 CM
SÉRIGRAPHIE EN BICHROMIE
GRANDE-BRETAGNE
1996/2004

"YOU ARE HERE" POSTER
MICHAEL JOHNSON
147.3 x 101.6 CM
2 COLOUR SCREENPRINT
UK
1996/2004

AFFICHES
SERVICE-CONSEIL PAPIER MCNAUGHTON
A0, LITHOGRAPHIE EN QUADRICHROMIE
GRANDE-BRETAGNE
1995

POSTERS
MCNAUGHTON PAPER ADVISORY SERVICE
A0, 4 COLOUR LITHO
UK
1995

From A4 folded samples to 8 page parallel over and outer folds, we can supply you **dummies** for your presentations

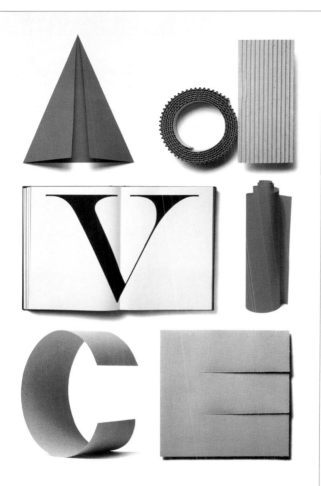

We're here to give you **advice** on all areas related to paper,
which to choose and which grades are suitable for your job

[DESIGN D'INTERACTION, DESIGN INTERNATIONAL]
IMAGES DU SITE INTERNET DU DESIGN COUNCIL
CARTES POSTALES A6, IMAGES DU SITE
GRANDE-BRETAGNE
2003/2004

INTERACTION DESIGN, INTERNATIONAL DESIGN
DESIGN COUNCIL WEBSITE IMAGES
A6 POSTCARDS, WEB IMAGES
UK
2003/2004

AFFICHE « R »
EXPOSITION [26 LETTRES]
BRITISH LIBRARY
152,4 x 101,6 CM
SÉRIGRAPHIE MONOCHROME
GRANDE-BRETAGNE
2004

"R" POSTER
26 LETTERS EXHIBITION
BRITISH LIBRARY
152,4 x 101,6 CM
1 COLOUR SCREENPRINT
UK
2004

designergueulsap / 036 / JOHNSON BANKS

So, if a brand *isn't* a logo and it's *not* a strapline and it's *not* a set of design guidelines, *what is it* exactly?

COUVERTURE
DE LA BROCHURE
PROMOTIONNELLE
DE BRITISH TELECOM
21 x 21 CM
LITHOGRAPHIE EN
QUADRICHROMIE
GRANDE-BRETAGNE
1996

BT BRAND MANUAL
COVER
BT
21 x 21 CM
4 COLOUR LITHO
UK
1996

[HORLOGE DES ICÔNES
BRITANNIQUES]
BRITISH COUNCIL
CERCLE DE 37 CM
DE DIAMÈTRE
HORLOGE
LITHOGRAPHIÉE EN
QUADRICHROMIE
GRANDE-BRETAGNE
1998

BRITISH ICONS CLOCK
BRITISH COUNCIL
37 CM CIRCLE
4 COLOUR LITHO
CLOCK FACE
UK
1998

designergußsap / 036 / JOHNSON BANKS

99

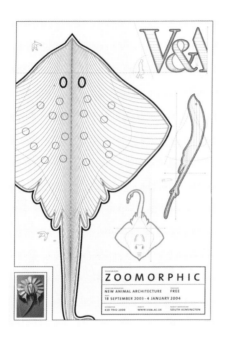
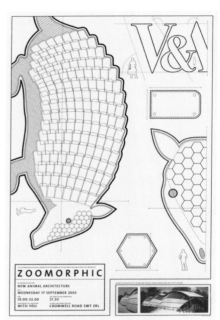

AFFICHE POUR LA CONFÉRENCE
« THE MODERN POSTER »
MICHAEL JOHNSON
152,4 x 101,6 CM
LITHOGRAPHIE MONOCHROME
GRANDE-BRETAGNE
1999

"THE MODERN POSTER"
LECTURE POSTER
MICHAEL JOHNSON
152.4 x 101.6 CM
1 COLOUR LITHO
UK
1999

LOGOS DES DIFFÉRENTES SECTIONS DE LA
NATIONAL FILM AND TELEVISION SCHOOL
A4
LITHOGRAPHIE EN QUADRICHROMIE
GRANDE-BRETAGNE
1994

NFTS DEPARTMENT LOGOS
NATIONAL FILM AND TELEVISION SCHOOL
A4
4 COLOUR LITHO
UK
1994

The Modern Poster

A REVIEW OF CONTEMPORARY POSTER DESIGN BY MICHAEL JOHNSON, JOHNSON BANKS

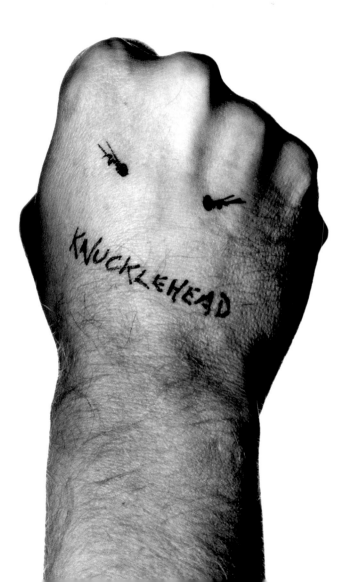

IDENTITÉ VISUELLE
SOCIÉTÉ DE PRODUCTION DE FILMS
KNUCKLEHEAD
A5, CARTES DE VISITE, AFFICHES A3
LITHOGRAPHIE EN BICHROMIE
GRANDE-BRETAGNE, 2004

CORPORATE IDENTITY
KNUCKLEHEAD FILM PRODUCTION
A5, BUSINESS CARDS, A3 POSTERS
2 COLOUR LITHO
UK
2004

Knucklehead

Unit 22-23
    Archer Street Studios
    10-11 Archer Street
    London W1D 7AZ

Tel: 0207 292 7950
Fax: 0207 734 7584
www.knucklehead.uk.com

MATTHEW BROWN

Knucklehead

Unit 22-23 Archer Street Studios
10-11 Archer Street
London W1D 7AZ

Tel: 0207 292 7950
Fax: 0207 734 7584
Mobile: 07768 404747

Email:
MATTHEW@KNUCKLEHEAD.uk.com

Registered address
26 Poor, 1-3 Leather Street, London W1S 6AE
Company registration No 179 313

Knucklehead Unit 22/23 Archer Street Studios 10-11 Archer Street
London W1D 7AZ Tel 0207 292 7950 Fax 0207 734 7584
www.knucklehead.uk.com

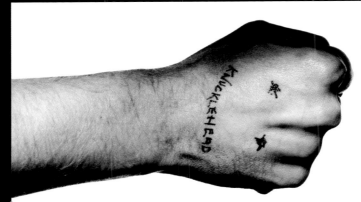

Knucklehead Unit 22/23 Archer Street Studios
10-11 Archer Street London W1D 7AZ
Tel 0207 292 7950 Fax 0207 734 7584
www.knucklehead.uk.com

EXPOSITION « WORDS AND PICTURES »
CREATION GALLERY, GINZA
JAPON
2004

"WORDS AND PICTURES" EXHIBITION
CREATION GALLERY, GINZA
JAPAN
2004

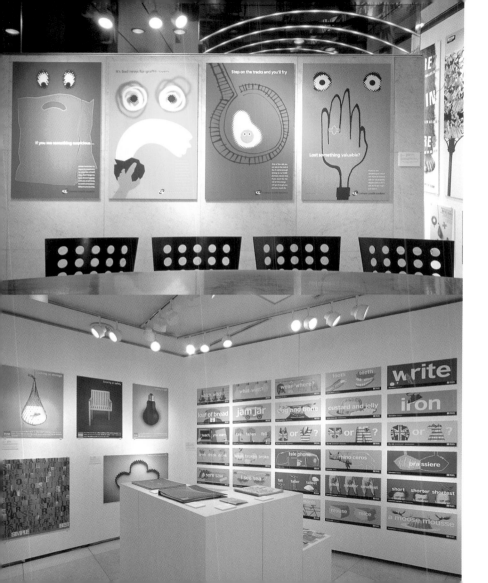

IDENTITÉ VISUELLE D'ANGEL
CONSULTATION PSYCHOLOGIQUE
POUR TOXICOMANES
AFFICHES A1
LITHOGRAPHIE MONOCHROME
GRANDE-BRETAGNE
2003

CORPORATE IDENTITY
ANGEL DRUG COUNSELLING SERVICE
A1 POSTERS
1 COLOUR LITHO
UK
2003

Vein?

Angel
Drug Services

Angel Drug Services offers:
Needle exchange
Confidential support
Advice and information
Treatment and care
Referrals
Support for family and friends

Visit Angel Drop-in at
33a Caswell Rd, Angel EC1
1.00–5.00pm Monday–Friday
6.00–9.00pm Tuesday & Thursday evenings
www.angeldrug.org.uk
Freephone 0800 169 2679

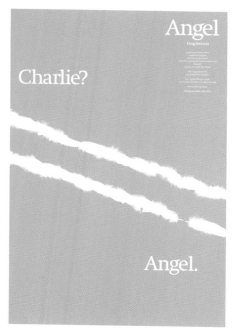

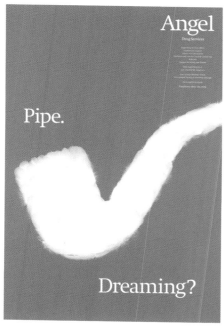

Angel

Drug Services

Angel Drug Services offers:
Confidential support
Advice and information
Treatment and care
Referrals
Support for family and friends

Visit Angel Drop-in at
332c Goswell Rd, Angel EC1

2.00–5.00pm Monday–Friday
6.00–9.00pm Tuesday & Thursday evenings

www.angeldrug.org.uk

Freephone 0800 169 2679

Speeding? Fine.

LANDFLEX

IDENTITÉ VISUELLE LANDFLEX
SOCIÉTÉ DE PLACEMENT LAND
LOGOS, TYPOGRAPHIE NUMÉRALE
GRANDE-BRETAGNE
2002/2003

LANDFLEX CORPORATE IDENTITY
LAND SECURITIES
LOGOS, NUMERALS
UK
2002/2003

The hole in the ozone layer has moved

CAMPAGNE CONTRE LE RÉCHAUFFEMENT
CLIMATIQUE
AFFICHES A0, LITHOGRAPHIE EN BICHROMIE,
EMPORTE-PIÈCE
GRANDE-BRETAGNE
2001

GEORGE BUSH KYOTO TREATY POSTER
CAMPAIGN AGAINST CLIMATE CHANGE
A0 POSTERS
2 COLOUR LITHO, DIE-CUT
UK
2001

Japan

Design Partners has endorsed a 3-year strategic plan in Japan. A scoping report was commissioned in 2002 and was written by Martin Darbyshire (tangerine product design and direction), Neil Hushtorth (Citygate Lloyd Northcroft) and Alison Scott (Export Promoter, Japan Unit at UK Trade & Investment).

Overview

Japan and the UK have many things in common. Both are a collection of islands, combine monarchy with democracy, have imperial pasts and strong traditions of craft-based businesses. They have both faced challenges to reinvent themselves, having had strong manufacturing sectors, albeit at different times. That challenge has never been more acute for Japan than right now. The country is currently going through a prolonged recession and major restructuring of the relationships between government, banks and businesses of all sizes are at varying stages of completion.

The Japanese have very clear ideas of what they want and very often whom they are prepared to buy it from. They have a reputation for being shrewd buyers of the original and the

unique, making their decisions quickly and enthusiastically. Without originality as part of 'the offer', UK design businesses will be less attractive. This coupled with the 'buyer' culture means it is not easy to sell to the Japanese. In fact, this report could be sub-titled 'By Invitation Only.' An important factor in winning new business therefore lies in knowing how to get invited in the first place.

There is common heritage between the two cultures but it would be wrong to think that this gives them a special 'inside track' to winning business in Japan. Japanese businesses' have a keen interest in innovation and winning in global markets. They will buy what they need from wherever they can find the best. 'Britishness' is not necessarily an attractive differentiator of UK consultancies; being genuinely international is.

Recent Events

Designer Makers – Crafts Council
In April 2003, the Crafts Council took a mission of designer-makers to Japan. The overall aim was to present a balanced overview of the contemporary British crafts and applied arts sector, improve contacts and international networks, generate opportunities for individuals and to continue to develop an understanding of the market potential.

Sixteen participants took part in the mission, including James Donald of Pick One, the winner of the 'British Crafts in Japan Award', sponsored by UK Trade & Investment at Chelsea Crafts Fair 2002.

In addition to the Mission Group, the two Crafts Officers used the opportunity of the Outward Mission to bring a group of Crafts Curators to Japan with the aim of supporting international cultural exchange and trade. The objectives of this group were to:

- give British Crafts Curators an introduction and overview of contemporary craft practice in Japan

- to establish contact with potential exhibition and project partners
- to meet makers, curators, arts managers and development professionals
- to support collaboration and dialogue between the curators' group and the makers' group.

James Donald won a number of commissions while in Tokyo. Fiona Hutchinson has just launched her tapestry exhibition in Tokyo, which will also tour to Kyoto and both Eileen Goldsmith and Lee Dalby have received commissions.

Digital Media Mission – August 2003
August 2003 saw the British Council take out a number of designers to the Onedot2ero Festival. The mission concluded that there were specific opportunities for British creatives offering services to the Japanese advertising sector.

Incoming Press Visit
Nikkei is Japan's leading design business publication, Design Partners endorsed the funding of an inward visit from Nikkei's Deputy Editor during the 2003 London Design Festival. This resulted in over 20 pages of editorial across 3 features in November 2003, December 2003 and January 2004.

UK ACTIVITIES

Events/publications supported by Design Partners and UK Trade & Investment in the UK include the following:

British Design Initiative launched its *Design Export and Government Who's Who*. This annual publication is a comprehensive guide to support services, grants and subsidies provided to support designers' export activities by UK Trade & Investment, British Embassies, Business Links and Design Bodies. It includes all key contact points and tips on how best to use the service, plus contact details for all major agencies and departments with an interest in the design industry including the Design Council, British Council, Department for Culture, Media and Sport (DCMS) and a full address list of all British embassies, Business Links and Ministers' offices.

The Design Trust revised its *Business Start-Up Guide for Designers*. The *Business Start-Up Guide 2003* is aimed specifically at designers who want to start their own business but find the prospect daunting. It covers the main topics that a fledgling business must address, and provides continuous signposting to business support agencies and services. It is also an information resource that lists useful websites and publications. A complimentary copy of the 60-page guide is available to download as a .pdf from www.designtrust.co.uk

The launch of the new *Design-Nation Catalogue*, which now includes 130 designers selected by professionals, took place on 25 September 2003 at 100%. Design. UK Trade & Investment part-sponsored the reception and invited commercial officers from British embassies, and the Foreign & Commonwealth Office brought an international press group. Also present were buyers, gallery owners, design organisations, representatives of City livery companies and interested members of the public. www.designnation.co.uk is now available in French, German, Italian and Spanish.

2003 saw the first *World Creative Forum* and *London Design Festival*. UK Trade & Investment and the British Council worked with the organisers to ensure vital international participation by supporting a series of launch events overseas and inviting a number of delegates to London in September.

In 2004, UK Trade & Investment will be sponsoring *The UK Trade & Investment Export Award* at the DBA Design Effectiveness Awards. The award will be presented to the most effective piece of work undertaken by a British business for an overseas client.

REGIONAL ACTIVITIES

Design Partners recognises that it needs to work more closely with Regional Development Agencies. As such, it has started a series of formal, regular meetings with International Trade Advisors and Business Link Advisors to encourage synergy in export strategies, share best practice and incorporate regional priorities into the national overview.

UK
PRESIDENCY
OF THE EU
2005

RAPPORT ANNUEL
DESIGN PARTNERS
A4
LITHOGRAPHIE EN
QUADRICHROMIE
GRANDE-BRETAGNE
2004

DESIGN PARTNERS
ANNUAL REVIEW
A4
4 COLOUR LITHO
UK
2004

LOGO
POUR LA PRÉSIDENCE
BRITANNIQUE DE
L'UNION EUROPÉENNE
MINISTÈRE
BRITANNIQUE
DES AFFAIRES
ÉTRANGÈRES
GRANDE-BRETAGNE
2005

LOGO
UK PRESIDENCY OF
THE EU
FOREIGN OFFICE
UK
2005

AWARDS / **PRIX**

8 pencils from Design and Art Direction (D&AD) including one gold (black pencil) + approximately 45 entries in the annual since 1991 • 1 Gold and 1 Silver cube from the Art Directors Club of New York + 4 distinctive merits, 3 design distinctions from American *I-D* magazine, 9 Design Week Best of Category Awards and 1 best of Show, 2 Millennium Products, 2 Design Effectiveness Awards • 25 posters held in the permanent design collection of the Victoria and Albert Museum • 1st most creative UK Design Company, Design Week Surveys 1999 & 2004 • Featured in the Design Week Hot 50 most important people in design 2003 and 2004 • Selected as one of the 10 best graphic designers in the UK by *The Independent* newspaper, 2003

EXHIBITIONS / **EXPOSITIONS**

Jeans Shop Ginza – Creation Gallery Tokyo, 2005
Communicate: *Independent British Graphic Design since the sixties* – Barbican Gallery, 2004-2005 – Guangzhou Museum of Art China, 2005
Words and Pictures, *the design work of Michael Johnson + johnson banks* – Creation Gallery Tokyo, 2004
Somewhere Totally Else, *European Design Biennial* – Design Museum, 2003
Rewind - *40 years of Design and Advertising* – Victoria and Albert Museum, 2002-2003
The Power of the Poster – Victoria and Albert Museum, 1998
D&AD awards exhibitions – 1991, 1993, 1997, 1999, 2002, 2003, 2004, 2005

INVOLVEMENT

D&AD President, 2003 • D&AD Education Chairman, 2001-2002 • D&AD Committee member, 1999-2003 • D&AD member since 1991 • Design Week Awards Chairman, 1998-1999 • External examiner, Glasgow School of Art, Ba Visual Communications • Visiting tutor, Kingston University, Central St Martins • Re-validation committee member, Royal College of Art Communications course, 1998 • Visiting lecturer: Kingston University, Nottingham University, Northumbria University, Middlesex University, Falmouth College of Art, Glasgow School of Art

PUBLICATIONS

As author:

Problem Solved: a primer in design and communication, Phaidon Press, 2002

As contributor:

The Education of a Typographer, Allworth Press, 2004

Rewind - 40 years of design and advertising, Phaidon Press, 2002

Featured in:

A history of Graphic Design, Meggs, 2005 • *Colour Design Workbook*, Rockport, 2005 • *20 years Creation Gallery*, G8, 2005 • *Communicate: Independent British Graphic Design since the sixties*, Laurence King, 2004 • *Logo Design Workbook*, Rockport, 2004 • *Size Matters*, Rotovision, 2004 • *Thames & Hudson Dictionary of Graphic Design + Designers*, Thames & Hudson, 2003 • *RSVP*, Rotovision, 2003 • *What is Graphic Design?*, Rotovision, 2002 • *Identify*, Rotovision, 2002 • *Graphic Originals*, Rotovision, 2002 • *The Graphics Book*, D&AD Mastercraft series, 2002 • *Experimental Packaging*, Rotovision, 2001 • *Experimental Formats*, Rotovision, 2000 • *New Design London*, Rockport, 1999 • *Typography*, Rotovision, 1999 • *A smile in the Mind*, Phaidon Press, 1996 • *The Best in Catalogue Design*, Quarto, 1994 • *D&AD Annual*, 1991-1994, 1996-2005

CREDITS

pp. 12-15: Michael Johnson, Harriet Devoy, Sarah Fullerton, Kath Tudball • pp. 16-19: Michael Johnson, Luke Gifford, Kath Tudball • pp. 20-21: Michael Johnson, Harriet Devoy, photography Piers North • p. 22: Michael Johnson • p. 23: Michael Johnson • pp. 24-25: Michael Johnson, Chris Wigan • pp. 26-27: Michael Johnson, Luke Gifford, Sarah Fullerton • pp. 28-29: Michael Johnson, David Jones, photography Mike Parsons • pp. 30-31: Michael Johnson, Luke Gifford, Sarah Fullerton • pp. 32-33: Michael Johnson, photography Dave Stewart • pp. 34-35: Michael Johnson, Sarah Fullerton, photography Phil Gatward • pp. 36-38: Michael Johnson, Andrew Ross, Sarah Fullerton, photography Kevin Summers • p. 40: Michael Johnson, David Jones • p. 41: Michael Johnson, Kath Tudball, Julia Woollams • p. 42: Michael Johnson • p. 43: Michael Johnson • pp. 44-45: Michael Johnson • p. 46: Michael Johnson • p. 47 top: Michael Johnson, Sarah Fullerton ; bottom: Michael

Johnson, Luke Gifford, Kath Tudball, Julia Woollams • pp. 48-49: Michael Johnson, Sarah Fullerton, photography David Sykes • pp. 50-51: Michael Johnson • p. 52: Michael Johnson, Kath Tudball, Julia Woollams, photography Kevin Summers • p. 53 left: Michael Johnson, Chris Wigan, production BBC ; right: Michael Johnson, Kath Tudball, Julia Woollams, photography Kevin Summers • p. 54: Michael Johnson, Luke Gifford, Kath Tudball • p. 55: Michael Johnson • p. 55 middle: Michael Johnson ; right: Michael Johnson, Julia Woollams • p. 56: Michael Johnson, Luke Gifford, photography Leon Steele • p. 57: Michael Johnson, photography Kevin Summers • p. 58: Michael Johnson, David Jones, photography Kevin Summers • p. 59: Michael Johnson, Zara Moore • pp. 60-61: Michael Johnson • pp. 62-63: Michael Johnson, David Jones, photography Kevin Summers • pp. 64-65: Michael Johnson, Andrew Ross, typographers The Foundry • pp. 66-67: Michael Johnson, photography Martin Barraud • p. 68: Michael Johnson • p. 69: Michael Johnson, Harriet Devoy • pp. 70-71: Michael Johnson, Modelmaker Wesley West • pp. 72-73: Michael Johnson, Luke Gifford • p. 74: Michael Johnson, Luke Gifford • p. 75: Michael Johnson, Luke Gifford, photographer Martin Barraud • p. 76: Michael Johnson, photographer Martin Barraud • p. 77: Michael Johnson, Chris Wigan • pp. 78-79: Michael Johnson, Julia Woollams • p. 80-81: Michael Johnson, Julia Woollams, Paola Faoro, Joshua Leigh • pp. 82-83: Michael Johnson, Kath Tudball, Julia Woollams • pp. 84-85: Michael Johnson, Luke Gifford • pp. 86-87: Michael Johnson, Luke Gifford • p. 88: Michael Johnson, Harriet Devoy • p. 89: Michael Johnson, Harriet Devoy, type The Foundry • pp. 90-91: Michael Johnson • pp. 92-93: Michael Johnson, Luke Gifford, Nina Jenkins • pp. 94-95: Michael Johnson, Sarah Fullerton, photography Phil Gatward • pp. 96-97: Michael Johnson, Julia Woollams, illustrator Neal Fox • p. 98: Michael Johnson • p. 99: Michael Johnson, Chris Wigan • pp. 100-101: Michael Johnson, Sarah Fullerton • pp. 102-103: Michael Johnson, Kath Tudball, Julia Woollams • p. 104: Michael Johnson • p. 105: Michael Johnson, photographer Martin Barraud • pp. 106-107: Michael Johnson, Kath Tudball, photography Kevin Summers • pp. 108-109: Michael Johnson • pp. 110-113: Michael Johnson, Kath Tudball, photography Kevin Summers • pp. 114-115: Michael Johnson, Sarah Fullerton • pp. 116-117: Michael Johnson • p. 118: Michael Johnson, Julia Woollams • p. 119: Michael Johnson, illustrator Ross Cooper